Hell is a Bipolar Dystopia

Tarphy W. Horn

The screams were as infinite as the reasons.

—*Situation*

ISBN: 978-1-7373698-6-8
Printed in the USA

Visit the author at www.tarphywhorn.com

INTRODUCTION

When I was eleven or twelve, I began to suspect something was wrong with me. While classmates and friends could regulate their emotions, mine spiraled out of control. My moods alternated between euphoria, deep hopelessness, paranoia, and anger, combined with extreme impulsivity. I knew my habit of staying awake all night and crying hysterically wasn't normal, and I didn't know of anyone else who exercised relentlessly for three, four, or even five hours every single day, usually in the dark. I had so much energy that I couldn't shut myself down. I cried about everything, even in public. I started to self-harm; physical pain was the only thing that could draw my attention away from the dumpster fire burning in my head.

My mood swings became more severe as I went through my teenage years. I grew up in a small, conservative town where conformity was everything; I hated conformity and wanted no part of it. I wanted to make friends and be popular, but I also hated everyone—a strange dichotomy, for sure. The unpleasant and extremely stressful relationship I had with my mother did little to help stabilize my unhealthy thoughts.

When I learned about bipolar disorder (which was called manic depression back then) my relief was indescribable. I had every symptom (or characteristic, if you prefer). I finally knew what was "wrong" with me. There was nothing I could do about it, though. The stigma surrounding mental disorders back then was much worse than it is now. Therapy wasn't an option; instead, I channeled my bizarre, dark, and disturbing thoughts into poetry.

About the poems

The subjects of the poems in the first chapter vary greatly. The first poem is about an opportunistic ghost. There are also poems about homelessness, failed relationships, and hope amid chaos. "Disenfranchised Droplets" is about what water would say if water could speak. "Stained Glass Song" describes hearing a song with your entire mind (I strongly recommend you look up a condition called synesthesia, if you don't know what it is). "@the_unbreakable_angel" is a tribute to an online friend whose whereabouts are unknown: please note this one has graphic descriptions of war. "A World Apart" is a poem I wrote as a pre-teen for my Great-Grandmother who lived in Colorado.

The contents of the second and third chapters were written in my teenage years, when I was, at times, struggling to maintain sanity. They deal with suicidal ideation, emotional abuse, disordered thoughts, mania, euphoria, catatonia, homicidal ideation, and severe depression.

The chapter called *Emotional Fuckery* is about manipulation.

The fourth and seventh chapters are full of strange little tales that happen to rhyme (mostly) and have very little to do with reality. "Free Intuitive Exercise" is from a kind of meditation session where you write whatever words come to you.

Chapter 5, *A Few Words About Words,* is just that: a bit about writing and reading.

"Battle" is a short, true narrative of two experiences I had after having surgery. It's not poetry, but it felt right to add it to this collection.

If you've made it this far and haven't been scared off, you're in for a wild ride!

THROUGH UNBLINKING
EYES

Escapee

Behind the abandoned, decrepit garage,
beneath where the sapphire sky
bled into cobalt,
above where our feet fell upon crunching leaves
(fiery orange, red, and brown),
in a tiny, dying, desolate town,
long since forgotten by progress and time . . .

that's where my cousin and I found the ghost.

It's no wonder, really,
that there'd be a few escapees from the gathering of
tombstones just up the road.

This one took a liking to Grandpa's big satellite dish
(the old kind from the eighties, planted in the
ground, giant and intimidating to the eyes of a
child).

The ghost said the dish helped him channel the
signals from Space,
to increase his energy flow.

No wonder Grandpa's TV reception was bad!

I know now, years later,
somewhere,
that ghost is basking in energy
siphoned from Wi-Fi and smart phones.

Shoes

The beggar studies the passers-by
who take extreme care to avert their eyes
They can't let their anonymity be relinquished
They don't want to admit their privilege
God forbid they be expected to change
their lifestyle
their thinking
society
anything.
God forbid they forfeit
or offer
one bit of comfort.
They are entitled
They are deserving
They are the people preserving
society
running the
world
turning the
wheels
The elite
The important
believe they matter the most
They are too busy to stop.

They assure themselves:
That begger wants money for booze or drugs
He's lazy, they think
He could be working
(even though he has no address or skills)
(even though he is disabled and sick).
They decide, *he must be crazy,*
so they can logically fear for their safety
and have an excuse to dismiss him
and believe he does not deserve food
or time.

A homeless girl struggles every day,
every hour,
to carry her dingy green backpack
to carry her guilt
her depression, disgust
her self-hatred. She knows her negligence
destroyed people's lives.

She casts a wary glance as she walks by the beggar.
She digs in her pockets
comes up with a couple of crumpled up dollars
and offers them up.

"Take a bus to St. Mary's shelter," she whispers,

"before the beds fill. It's going to rain tonight."

He can see she is starving

and shivering

and tells her, with kindness,

"I can't take this.

Use it to go get some soup."

She laughs bitterly

says no

says she doesn't deserve it

says she's schizophrenic

and an alcoholic.

She went to work drunk, crushed a man with a

forklift

and hasn't worked since.

The fingers of clenched fists

dig deep, bloody crescents into her palms.

She doesn't notice, but he does.

He accepts the money and tells her to talk to her

sponsor.

She makes him a promise they both know she won't

keep

He thanks her for the bus fare

but slips the money into her backpack

as she walks away.
"I like your shoes," he calls as she's parting.
She turns and smiles
but just keeps on walking.
He knows he won't see her again
and feels an inexplicably deep sense of loss.

The world keeps on turning
The passers-by pretend not to notice
that someone with nothing
tried helping a stranger
Reminding themselves of the inherent danger,
they keep on walking without feeling guilty.
At night they drink wine, take valium, pass out
on soft pillows and expensive sheets
in warm beds and sleep soundly.

Pensive

A child in a field

all alone with memories

sees

a lifeless tree,

its colors on the ground.

The sun beats down,

but she is cold

filled with miseries untold

and haunted by a dream that can't unfold.

Countdown

Eight hours stretch out before me.

♦

I search for meaning in numbers, but meaning
eludes me.
I mistakenly download
the "clean lyrics" version
of a new song.
Such a vile thing shouldn't exist.
I feel angry and cheated.
I look up to slowly face the soulless face of the
Clock.
It smirks and tells me seven hours remain.

♦

Coffee gets cold very quickly, I've learned.
Outside the sky is as grey as the words that demand
my attention.
Important words to a few people, but none of them
matter to me.
A spider rappels down the wall. I envy it. It has a
purpose.
Six hours remain.

♦

I could go for a walk after work if I lived somewhere
warm. But I don't, so I settle for walking into other
offices looking for candy.

No one will share (at least, not with me).

A vast stretch of boredom descends upon me.

Five hours remain.

♦

I desperately seek an escape from the doldrum.

Maybe I could write a novel, I think. I could get
famous and go on a talk show.

But I loathe daytime TV.

So I keep looking at these words and numbers.

They all blur together like dense, silver fog.

Maybe I could start a blog?

Unlikely, and four more hours remain.

♦

I had a past life. I lived in a castle. In a future life,
I'll exist as light spreading deeper and deeper and
deeper through the cacophony of stars.

In this life I'm stuck with

these numbers that never add up

and three hours remain.

♦

My phone breaks its long spell of silence. I trade
words with someone from Brooklyn. I wonder what

her office looks like. Maybe she counts down time, too.

Two hours remain.

♦

Gossip comes drifting my way. I slink away from its slippery tendrils. My coworkers take my disinterest for selfish aloofness. These people see me every day but don't know me at all.

One very long hour remains.

I think I might slip off my shoes. At least then my toes will know freedom.

Emergence

First there's emergence:
a collection of music notes escaping from chaos
creating a song,
oil paints flying across the room and transforming a
canvas into a masterpiece,
words forming sentences
paragraphs
pages
stories.
Birth.
Then !suddenly
!sharply
everything freezes.
Evil hatches
and art's shoved aside.

Next there's existence:
a traveler starting a journey,
feeling all there is to feel
Experiencing
rain
human connection
grass between toes
betrayal

screaming

the smell of fresh paint

the indifference of cats

fried squash

shame

soft pillows

privilege

devastation

runny nose

snowcapped mountains

touching velvet

touching fire

starvation

cerulean blue

terror

alcoholism

exaltation

darkness.

Every action taken

mixes the notes into either

a symphony

or a discordant roar

The traveler

can paint an ornate masterpiece,

or scribble on paper, then crumple it up,

can write either

a timeless bestseller

or a litany of angry nonsense

It all stems from one choice the traveler makes:

Creation?

Destruction?

Damnation?

or Nothing?

If wisdom prevails, there can be evolution:

the traveler must look up

take a chance

fly

share the song

and change everything.

The Charmed Ones

Beautiful yet forgettable faces
watching each other in a better place
a safe space from which to watch the world burn
a safe place to spin
when the earth finally fails to turn.

But in spite of the magic utopia they've created,
they are fated to float through their lives without
leaving a trace, casting a shadow, or impacting
anything,
not mattering, not helping
discovering nothing, uncovering, solving, creating
nothing
of consequence.

The charmed ones are not held accountable for
destruction, misinformation, sickness, or failings.
They don't want to be copied or followed,
yet they want to be followed and copied.

Some others, those who aren't charmed ones,
misguided and desperate people,

people with dreams of rising from the ranks of
destitution to a world where they'll no longer
matter;
their dreams are stalled
by the words coming out of the mouths
of the charmed ones.

Half-finished Paintings

Half-finished paintings
drift slowly from sanity,
giving up hope as their creators age

Laughing maniacally,
mostly forgotten in some locked-up studio,
maybe an attic.
Propped against walls,
tossed into chairs,
hoping that someday they'll grace someone's hall

Some simply abandoned, left naked;
paint splashed on canvas and left to be finished
when "someday" arrives.

The colors are screaming, but
no one is listening.

They reach and they struggle
and try to grab on
But they can't quite achieve
tangibility, substance

They have no value

until they're completed;
the artists don't care.

They will stay hungry

They will stay waiting

No one pays attention
to half-finished paintings.

Perspective

It doesn't matter

if you're on top of the world

if all the action

takes place on the ground.

Word Pollution

Word pollution

fractures our souls:

Every tongue spewing hate

Every ear building walls

Every finger attacking in cyberspace

Word pollution

poisons the earth

as deadly as cyanide

and inside all of us.

The American Way

I wake up on January 3, 2020.
People are panicking about World War III on social
media
and I think,
I did NOT live through the Cold War
only to deal with this shit AGAIN.
I think about the Star-Spangled Banner:
the rockets' red glare
the bombs bursting in air
and think, I don't want to see that in my skies.
Innocent people have seen it, of course, and many
more will,
so that evil people do, too.
I can't prevent it
from happening here
any more than I could've prevented
getting nuked in the 80's.
Though it's something I fear
I can't change it.
I can only write about it
until I can't.
Social media
what a clusterfuck.
Thank God for it.

***

He stayed home from work today, because there are
Things To Do.
I'm briefly, shamefully, naturally thankful that
everyone in my immediate family is too unhealthy
to be drafted,
even if the military becomes desperate.

Today, I will pay cash for ammo.
It's the American Way.

I'll go stock up on bottled water
before other panicking citizens clear the shelves in
Walmart, like they did during the dystopian horror
of the bleak days and weeks after 9/11.

I call my parents and tell them to fill their car with
gas, because gas prices are likely to soar.
At least now I've done something
that gives me a sense of power in the face of
helplessness.

They say war today won't just be nuclear. It will be
chemical. biological. electronic.

Will it all end in a Zombie Apocalypse? Will we all die from the Superflu?

Maybe not.
Maybe aliens will intervene.
Maybe humans suck that much.

Redacted

THE

TRUTH

MUST

BE

REVEALED

WE

MUST

ACT

NOW

WE

MUST

UNITE

WHILE

THERE'S

STILL

TIME

TO

STOP

THE

INSANITY

Just Truth

No heaven hovers above.
No hell looms below.
No destiny rules decisions.
Fate isn't a reason for all this derision.

No freedom, chains, or chances.

Beauty is not Truth! only an opinion.

No evil versus good. Evil and good are not Truth.

No compliance required
for deafening whispers
demanding compliance.

Identities fought for
Identities bought
Identities some won't accept
and won't recognize;
regardless,
Identities are Truth.

Authorities with no spine supporting their self-
serving, self-righteous decisions

and rants
Bought and sold and no longer sure of their own
opinions or stance.
They operate in a trance, with no concept of morals,
No concept of Truth.

Morals, subjective
no right or wrong.
Right and wrong are not Truth.

No miracles.
They were Truth until they left with God.

Laws? Rules? Social norms?
Yes
Guardian Angels?
Distinct possibility.
Light and Grace,
religion erased
to search for spirituality.
Losing is Truth.
Losing is gaining.

No end and no beginning. No when. Only now.
No manifest destiny, preordination

No blessings.
They withdrew from existence when God fled.
No future.
No forgiveness, forgetting.
Not anymore.

The transgressions are many;
no redemption from depravity

Nothing hides in the closet
or under the bed

Sometimes, Beauty is truth.

No immortality
No salvation.

Only
chemicals
reacting.

Stained Glass Song

Drumbeats forming inside the shadows
dance upon wavering ground
like thundering hooves stampeding
or echoes of baby feet pattering.

Notes from the keyboard, pastel clouds
mumbling gently right to left,
like angelic lyrics
scribed in Enochian,
lyrics that blaze like a stained-glass song.

The bouncing sound radiates.
Magic guitar sounds
glow, overflow, rich and round
in the sky,
curling all over, smoking and
learning to fly.

Wisps of gold chiming percussion
lips randomly kissing the air.
Her voice: shining light shooting skyward
Her mouth firing comets of sound
The words are so fierce and yet fragile.
Rich colors dwell inside tones

Some colors nameless
Some not existing in nature
A background of barbed silk and ice

Medieval swords swinging
The deepest shades of mahogany
melting.
Cohesion from chaos, and healing
explained, understood.
Perfect communication from voices awry.
Dissipating, the blurry edges describe no beginning
or end.
They flow freely, dragging me along for the ride,
and I'll give it all for four minutes.

As the fire burns down to dark embers,
the soul shatters back into pieces.
The wholeness it found in the music
burns out with a sigh.

Sand

Overused memories, generally
still invoke strains of pleasant nostalgia
as sunlight lays low on the glassy surface of
perfect beaches.

Fiery images and flaming emotions
Dealing with stress and depression
Tides flow in, making sandcastles crumble
as moonlight caresses the water
and struggles to beam onto shrinking expanses of
perfect beaches.

Past experiences struggle to cross the waves
without getting swept away violently
by unseen currents disguised as pure, inviting
islands
where damp toe-prints serve as memorials.

The colors of sunset
explode and paint the ocean.
The bonfires cast their smoky scent,
And the crystalline sand records it all.

@the_unbreakable_angel

I didn't know she lived in Kyiv until she posted the
videos of
animals rescued, a kitten's paw pushing against a
human palm
babies rescued, their tiny bodies filthy but
breathing
the elderly rescued, sometimes, incredibly, without
a scratch on them.

First responders, friends, families, neighbors,
strangers spending hours or days digging, calling
out, hoping to pull someone out of the rubble.
Sometimes saving a child.
Sometimes finding only an arm with debris-coated
fingers, reaching out futilely to be saved from a
dark, crushing, suffocating, terrifying, infuriating,
meaningless, unnecessary, and unfair death.

She posted before-and-after pictures of buildings
destroyed. Land destroyed.
Landmarks destroyed.
An unexpectedly beautiful country
decimated

Thousands of people, packed onto streets, shoulder
to shoulder, with no room to move or breathe or
live
Miles of cars filling roads as desperate souls fled
their homes,
homes lost to hatred and the worst of humanity
homes lost to drones in the sky, programmed with
orders
and drones on the ground, brainwashed by orders
mindlessly following,
some consciously enjoying
reducing those homes to small piles of rubble.

Every memory built by Ukrainians
spread across miles and miles of freshly formed
Nothingness.

I watched every video @the_unbreakable_angel
posted
saw a doctor make a prosthetic leg for a donkey
saw neighbors help neighbors and
risk their lives to save pets

I wondered how these victims who refused to be
victims kept their humanity

while staring down the devil, every single day.
I wondered how they kept their sanity
listening to air raid sirens blaring and bombs
exploding and structures collapsing;
constant, unending, unfiltered noise.

I wondered when humanity lost its humanity.

Her social media followers asked
@the_unbreakable_angel why she chose to stay.
We offered repeatedly to send her money so she
could leave;
even those struggling promised to find a way to
help.
A few friends in Europe offered her space in their
homes
as we all begged her to flee to safety.

With unfathomable strength, pride, ferocity, she
said she refused to be chased from her home
from her friends
from her family
her life
even after a missile flew over her head while she
walked home with her sister

even after falling to the ground in her kitchen when
the building across from hers exploded, rumbling
as it collapsed.
She'll suffer from serious PTSD her whole life, I
thought. *How could anyone ever hope to recover
from living through such horror?*

And still, her compassion was endless.

She posted about
catastrophic flooding in India
(where a villager collected cats in a basket to save
them from drowning);
She made sure people learned of
the plight of children enslaved in the Congo;
the suffering of the Syrian people;
the horrific sight of decomposed babies left
unburied in Gaza,
when relatives couldn't recover their bodies
or relatives were reduced to decomposed bodies
themselves
the children whose arms carried limp bodies
that once had belonged to their younger siblings,

the doctor who continued performing the surgery
he was performing while finding out his family had
just been blown to pieces

From peoples' expressions and even the animals'
sorrowful eyes,
we, scattered across the earth, learned the true
madness her people contended with
She shared horrors
never discussed on the mainstream news
Horrors too graphic to show to the public
too graphic to live through and still remain sane
but borne by people with no other choice or
alternative.

With wisdom far beyond her years
(people so young growing up so fast to survive in
hellish, dystopic ruins),
she instructed everyone to live a good life, to love
and be happy
and cultivate peace.

She hasn't posted for nine weeks
and three days
I check every day

but I'm certain
she won't post again.

In her last private message to me, she told me how
worried she was for her friends in America
dealing with all of the gun violence.

Manifesto

Without diversity, no evolution.

only stagnation.

Whispers in hallways and frantic discussions.

Education

on social media platforms

dangerous to corrupt corporations

corrupt politicians

So they introduce Bills to suppress information

Homelessness. Starvation.

Depression. Destruction. Societal breakdown.

Panic, frustration.

Social contracts eroded beyond repair

The sins of the elders will not be forgiven;

there is no time.

They'll ride with us into the nothingness.

Ruled by greed, instead of intelligence

No solving problems.

Everyone suffers.

Nature is screaming.

Resources depleted.

Ingredients, all, in a recipe for revolution.

Without empathy, no understanding

Never seeing a different perspective.

Racists emboldened.

Innocent people attacked so the rich get their way

can steal their land.

can steal their resources.

Hostages die in captivity.

Truth is selective, twisted by media,

who we've been trained and brainwashed to trust

and believe and accept

Blending what's real with gross propaganda.

Indoctrination

always their plan.

They demand mindlessness

pump out pollution

to poison our bodies and minds and souls

Hatred runs rampant. Diseases are planted.

We turn an exhausted blind eye to the needy.

But slowly, we're peeking out

from the mountains of toxic garbage

spewed by the one percent

and finding a

reason for revolution

Finding a way to ignite the unrest

Finding a way to voice our protests

Finding out our survival depends on

the inevitable revolution.

Failed Connection

Leave a message at the tone?

Okay, here it goes.

I don't know if you'll ever hear this,

or listen if you do. Maybe this isn't even your

number anymore. I just wondered,

Do you remember when I called you late that night?

We hadn't talked in years, but we made up for lost

time. You were smoking something, I was drunk on

rum and coke.

We talked for hours about our lives, our

disappointments, memories. We grieved for all the

dreams that somehow fell apart. I'm clearly not an

astronaut; you never made the Pros.

I told you how I worried when you shipped out to

Japan.

It was safer than Afghanistan,

safer than Iraq,

but still we were at war.

I kept the newspaper clipping with a picture of you

in uniform.

I don't know if he ever told you, but you made your

dad so proud when you followed in his footsteps

and became a Marine.

I'm proud, too.

I admit I claim a tiny bit of credit for helping raise you.

I remember going to the post office and sending you my grandma's old Bible with the black leather cover that closed with a zipper. Back then, I believed it would protect you. I think Grandma would've approved that I passed it on to you, although I doubt you read it.

That's okay. I've lost my faith, too.

When you told me you and Beth don't talk now, I was sad but not surprised. She's always gone her own direction, and I'm sure she's doing fine.

I miss her, too,

but I don't have her number anymore.

I hope someday you meet your niece and nephews. That girl you vaguely mentioned that you dated while you served? I don't need to know what happened or why you won't say her name. The way you talked I think she killed something inside you. I think she caused far more damage than a bullet, missile, IED or bomb could ever do.

I'd like to have a Word with her about breaking your heart. You deserve love, and I hope someday you heal and find someone who makes you happy.

I really hoped my kids could get to know you.

I'm just hoping that your demons didn't get you.
I don't think you've changed your number, but I
can't seem to reach you anymore.
But if you ever want to hang out, talk, grab some
lunch or toss around a football, you can call me at
this number.
Life's been crazy; there's so much I'd like to tell you.
Only this time, I'll be sober.
Well, I better go. If you call and I don't answer the
phone,
leave a message at the tone.

A Secret Name Everyone Knows

Ritualistic and pompous
lacking in substance
but thriving in power
The irony of the self-righteous,
(who only participate if it's convenient)
is not overlooked.

Their scholars look at the sky
but can't see the Universe.
Can't see the Dawning, and
don't care the planet is dying.

Sequestering progress,
threatened by free-thinking warriors.
They graffiti their bodies
with frightening adherence to ritual
They abhor the enlightened
They ignore the warnings
Their souls are screaming.
The *whole world* is screaming.
We must reach them, tell them as they glower,
Don't honor that make-believe power!
For all of our sakes, break free from captivity
Go reclaim your life

and walk through a field of sunflowers

Count flecks of gold in the ocean

feel what it's like to squish toes in the sand

Breathe in the magic of seeing the tundra

A different perspective exists at fourteen thousand
feet,

when looking at tiny but ancient life that's been
here

for ten thousand years

but has never had need

for the secret name everyone knows

Don't poison the dandelions because you think they
are weeds.

You can still enjoy the lawn,

if you accept that it now has more colors.

As Magic Dies

Would this have ended differently
if we were not constantly
stepping on top of each other?
Trampling through each other's space?

If we both were happy still
living in our own bodies?
If the fistful of time taking over
and punching us
had left less of an impact?

If cats
didn't constantly
knock shit all over the place
make messes
and pester
and multiply?

If stress didn't fill up
the buckets left sitting all over
to catch the drips
from the leaky ceilings
that represent our lives?

I hear wind laughing
through the cracks in our foundation
and if we are honest,
the structure wasn't that strong in the first place.

Now, looking at the boxes
containing the clutter
that once seemed so direly
needed, we try to summon the old spark
but somewhere along the road
that squeaky magic fell, died
I miss it, more than I'll ever miss you.

Disenfranchised Droplets

Filling up the fountain were the rejects from the
sea.

They formed the wrong reflection and the image
wasn't me.

Where once they'd lofted warships, now they slid
down dying leaves.

Once in time they filled the tides
but now, in silence, grieve.

So I filled my hands with water, and I threw it
toward the sky
and it climbed into the clouds
and it rained a lullaby

On returning to the ground,
resignation settled in
as the water spread across the earth and
disappeared within.

A World Apart

Eerie, misty mountain skies
softly sing sweet lullabyes
Majestic pine trees standing guard
watching over Time's backyard
Rivers rushing, filled with gold
spilling secrets yet untold.
Fragile ground untouched for years
Waterfalls weep mystical tears.
Jagged peaks covered with newfallen snow.
Sun sinks behind the valley below
Explosions of color light up the night sky
Fields of stars float silently by
Steep slopes bear witness to nature's rebirth
Clouds reach down and tickle the earth.
In this world apart, a world divine
A world forever locked in time.

INSIDE A MIND THAT
MISFIRES

The Last Mistake

Clouds slip over everything,
blanketing the hollow screams
Lights out, shades up in my room
letting in the dripping gloom.

Sky is clear now, sun is gold;
Outside lurks late autumn's ghost.
Depression sinks into my soul
into every crack and hole

Clouds return with faceless fog,
penetrate, expose the raw
and devastating final ache
I can't fight off the last mistake.

Fighting Off Madness

Worthless

(like a single shoe abandoned on the side of the road)

Pointless

(like waiting for roses to grow out of concrete)

Useless

(like opening car doors for ghosts)

Hopeless

(like expecting cats to start caring about anything that doesn't benefit them)

Reckless

(like voices careening through vacuums)

Aimless

(like shadows dissolving in darkness)

Monotonous

(like washing dishes each day)

Repetitive

(like washing dishes each day)

Ridiculous

(like gravity taking a day off)

Exhausting

(like trying to stand still on a treadmill)

Annoying

(like when the voices won't agree with each other)

Exhilarating

(like finding your name on an NSA watch list)

Upsetting

(like flushing your drugs)

Disastrous

(like leaving your fingerprints at the scene)

Difficult

(like finding new places to safely stash bodies)

Frustrating

(like improvising when the store's out of rat poison)

Challenging

(like evading an entire police squad)

Infuriating

(like getting sprayed in the eyes with mace)

In vain

(like pleading your case when you're caught in the act)

Depressing

(like pressing your fingers in ink)

Fighting off madness is worse than you think.

The Sun Sleeps

I am sunset orange on a dying world,
alone with frenzied thoughts

Inside my head, reality rots.
I am stilled by what I am not.

This hellish vacation
Has one consolation

I may be the absence of heat,
but at least I'm the focus of light.

The Other

The Other likes living so I'm forced to let her.
I am the core
but she is the center.

This ongoing fantasy may last forever
Depression begging my life to be better

Reality flows
to and from her
both ways
from inside the red velvet hallway
to outside.

The daze
in my eyes as
my mind slips into a phase
in another misunderstood realm of this place
which isn't real and can't exist
So why do I still feel
duality's gist?

More

Riding on beams of pale blue light,

streaming through dark corridors,

splitting the emptiness to fill either side,

(a temporary fix

but better than nothing),

struggling to be more than

a simple character dwelling forever in fantasy.

I am more than my diagnosis.

I am bear, I am wolf

owl and raven

gargoyle and mountain.

This dreamer's ideas

could fill an arena

I am more than a presence in nightmares

Potential bursts forth

A beacon that shatters the darkness

a guide that ends the wandering

through life's confusing abyss.

I am more than your expectations.

I could fill the whole world with an explorer's

lusting.

I'm more than a mind that misfires.

Reason

I hold my head high;
not to seem brave,
but to make gravity
fight for my tears.

Restless

Pinecones dropped from the majestic evergreen tree, accumulating in random piles specifically for her entertainment. The Girl deigned to watch. Wasps crawled over her bare feet, trying and failing to elicit a twitch from her toes. She absently mocked their failure.

Her consciousness streamed through the museum of Earth, speculating. Dreams leaked from her subconscious. She distractedly mourned their loss as they faded away.

She was restless.

The desperate ache of unrealized expectations seeped into her soul. Voices whispered to her from the Deep Edges, as her body sprawled across the golden wasteland. She plucked the dead stalks of weeds from their earthy graveyard.

Her exalted existence was sensed by everyone left behind in the shadows as Time lurched forward in jagged spurts. She used the Normals' admiration to help refuel her extinguished guiding light. Her replenished power allowed her to heroically drop the rope and rescue the stragglers dangling over the abyss. This ability was her birthright.

A wasp succeeded in stinging her toe. Fury replaced indifference; not because of the discomfort, but for the interruption of experiencing her fascinating misery. Visualizing the physical pain in her foot and encapsulating it in a cubical bubble, she pushed it from her mind to create space for her dark musings.

Trying to find solace in the familiar and far away, her essence traveled to the places she loved as a child. Disappointment again draped over her when she arrived and found herself outcast and replaced by new ideas. She no longer belonged in the places she considered home. Violent waves of anger and hurt threatened to smother her as she fought to free herself from the box.

As she had predicted, her mind overflowed with secret knowledge. She was fantastically lucky and blessed, and she understood this with amazing clarity. The Universe revealed its darkest secrets to her and her alone.

Other dimensions poured into hers and filled the empty spaces. Planets, blazing with rubies and carnelian and surrounded by moons of emeralds and sapphire, swirled through gold and silver flakes of cosmic dust. Opal and diamond stars twirled like ballet dancers on the theatrical stage of infinity.

Frantically she groped through the Veil to find the words to describe what she was seeing. The correct vocabulary eluded her. She scribbled furiously in The Notebook. Panicked, she poured words onto page after page, preserving the Truths of reality to share with humankind. The Experts would bow to her brilliance.

Upon rereading her writings to enjoy her cleverness, she was horrified to discover gibberish. The whispers from the Deep Edges had tricked her, and she'd fallen for the deception.

Ah well, she thought, this line of thinking required too much technical knowledge to produce a perfected work anyway.

The ability to engage her alter egos slipped away. Time was wasting, rushing away from her, and she was failing to fulfill her existence on the Plane Which She Controlled! The anger building up interfered and slammed and locked the doors to the room with the elegant prizes.

By the *GODS* she was *RESTLESS*!

***

The nurse came into the room where the girl sat, staring at the wall, unmoving. He shook his head, remembering the extensive medical records that speculated on the cause and treatment of her catatonia.

Such a waste. The doctors said she had an IQ of 170.

He found an area of skin untouched by the scars of self-harm. He rubbed a small area of her arm with alcohol and injected the usual cocktail of antipsychotics, mood stabilizers and tranquilizers.

Bipolar Dystopia

Inspired
to manifest my haunting goals

Bound
by paralyzing flavors fed into my soul

Forced
to glimpse a candy-tasting life

Forged
of bitter steel, like a dull-edged knife

Inundated
by the fear of failing

Violated
by the patriarchy that's prevailing

Bathed
in something larger than myself

Dreaming
of the precipice from which I'll launch myself

Frozen
in a secret private tragedy

Cursed
to be unfathomable and hungry

Free
in only daydreams and imaginings

Condemned
to live in Bipolar Dystopia.

Seeking Rhythm

I may find my rhythm
climbing angry gangly trees,
where knots provide the footholds
for my bare and clinging feet.

Fingers stripping bark away
to music out of sync;
memories of dazzling smiles
flash by me with a wink.

Branches crashing down—they're mine!
Still, further up I climb,
pulling strength from heartache
as I leave the dirt behind.

Oak, its roots a permanent
fixture beneath the ground;
those roots must grow deeper,
or my rhythm won't be found.

Soul Control

The weakness of the body and mind
are tolerated by a soul
in a few rare cases
when it senses something more.

Confessions

I am stressed,
blessed,
on my quest,
the epitome of zest!
I'm the grinning sunset in the west.

Okay I confess,
I failed the reality test.
With honesty, in truth,
I'm nothing but a mess.

I am distant and depressed,
distressed and oppressed,
expressive? Unexpressed.
Sometimes I'm possessed
and a guest in my own flesh.

My personality's recessed.
My mind, undressed.
I've regressed,
acquiesced,
and given up hope of being the best.
I am blatantly obsessed.
I'm freefalling through this mess

of hopelessness

faithlessness

never-ending restlessness.

I could not be coping less.

Harrowing!

Full blown cardiac arrest!

I need rest.

I'm still a guest in my own flesh,

in the midst of helplessness,

I drown in my duress.

Legacy

Crumbling walls
Warped vision, tears
Fake apologies falling
on uninterested ears

Failed conversation
Heated self-loathing
Red, twitching face
betrays my emotions

Fractured relationships
Screaming at darkness
Nightmares that linger
This is my legacy.

Diagnoses

Diagnoses
spoken garbage,
suffocating and exhausting,
words that I cannot pronounce,
suppositions that are wrong,
misdirecting,
a hindrance,
causing damage.

I've been told,
but we need labels!
Labels give Identity!
let our pain be Validated,
Recognized,
and let us get the Help we need!

But labels, diagnoses,
obliterate aspects of freedom,
block us from realizing our dreams,
steal our future,
lead us down an empty path with no beginning or
end,
leaving us with nothing but a stale word.
A reduction to nothing but a name on a list.

Your credibility ceases to exist.

My reflection shows no evidence of need

of all the chemicals they push on me.

Legal transformation into a zombie!

Words that I cannot pronounce.

It's a crutch I don't require.

Precious Monsters

I'm surviving
and the sun still goes on rising every day,
or so I've heard.

Looking back through all the pages in my
scrapbook of Psychosis, I find precious monsters.
So misunderstood.
And I wonder where the person that I've always
been
has gone.

Rolling laughter in the mirror
from my reflection—
Which of us resides in the mercury dimension?
I stare at two eyes I don't recognize.

Mind pollution
Devastation
Suffocation
Inexplicable.

My tears should drill into the earth,
make an impression,
but they land and bounce off granite.

I don't panic.

I will finally allow myself to mourn.

In my scrapbook of Psychosis

hiding deep within the pages

precious monsters knock the memories around.

Random ramblings resurface and then drown.

Under My Skull

Out of control
extreme concentration
incredible highs
unspeakable lows

So many times,
I've wanted to die.

Only once have I tried,
(and was blessedly denied).

All that I wanted
was just out of reach
All that I needed,
impossibly far
How could I be more alone?
Or Alive?
Some claim
my delusions are mist in the wind.
they know nothing of what goes on under my skin.
under my skull.

The only sympathetic
receivers, projectors,

live in my mind,
are but fleetingly real
in my fleeting reality.

So I lay here in darkness
listening
to the songs that remind me of the faraway places
that are home.

Mania

All of this gibberish
made so much sense
but thoughts are elusive and slippery.

I still catch a few ideas with clarity
Yes! they meet the requirements
and quench my frantic thirst to
proclaim...something.

No, not quite *frantic*.
Imperative.
Vital. Urgent.
Garbled words, Garbled thoughts,
A poison that must leave the body.

Damaging, ravaging,
Mania gets its way and toys with my brain.
I know later I'll pay, but not today.

What a mad machine
cranking out fevered, furious knowledge
doomed to be lost forever
Its only hope: knowledge forcing itself onto
someone

somewhere

anywhere

anyone

The need, evoked only in the clawed-up remains of
a single night

SUCH A SENSE OF IMMERSION

minds connecting, every thought touching, forming
an elite connection;

We,

our souls, our life force, our energy

all mix together, a deep sea of diamonds.

The rarest ones sparkle, as bright as a star.

The others are rough

Their strength—not enough.

Unwanted dilution

Pain is a welcome stimulation, a distraction
that draws my mind, finally, away.

Sudden panic

fraying knots on thinning rope

Something's missing!

Something's been taken!

Something

Really

Really

Important to me

Fucking *Vital!!!*

Where can I run?

Where should I be?

I've been blocked!

It's a waste of me!

I can't let this be

when I could rule Infinity.

Lament

I sit and watch the cars go by and wonder why.
Although I try to understand how life is planned
it utterly eludes me.

It's interesting how things that bring such
satisfaction
suddenly can fade away to yesterday
where they cease to exist.

Choice

The dark twisted image stared back at me
Its questioning eyes were full of deceit
After we woke from the torturous dream
on the blackest of black nights
when no one is free,
the multiple beings exclaimed,
My turn! Me!
I, the dominant, forced to retreat.
The pills were not helping!
Not helping me *be*!
And I was aware of me
hiding in me
If I punched the mirror, shattered the dream
shattered the trauma
the others could flee
If I turned away, let them take over
while I ran for cover
and huddled inside
then I could find peace.
Instead I chose anger.
I chose to be free.
In the end, I chose me.

Monster

Not that I'm beautiful
oh, but I wish
even a monster
would call to me longingly.

Cosmic Puzzle of Longing

The randomness all comes together, like some cosmic puzzle of longing assembled on Earth:

The pale, smothering ache of yearning

Strangers sewing anticipatory discord with golden needles

The boundless freedom of nightfall and star fields

Layers of music stacking together to form a song that drops on eager ears

Frying light, the shining grease illuminating a burden that should, but won't, stay hidden

Memories of events that are yet to happen

They all fit together, one cosmic puzzle assembled, connecting the dissonant hells of solitude and entanglement.

Adrift

My soul
the haunted memory
drifting on a silent sea
like a prisoner set free
who cannot bear to leave.

Blackened Abyss

I always knew it would be like this
Death, a great flowing blackened abyss.
Light in a tunnel of darkness
and *bliss!*
And a voice saying,
Nothing to fear!
The voice
invited my mind to invite it
inside
I resisted,
extinguished the light,
darkened the tunnel,
and deepened the voices
The fear invaded my mind
I saw I'd been tricked
I'd been wronged
I arrived at a closed door,
held shut by the dead.
I looked back for a key
The hallway was dark
The night was dark
not even a flashlight or a lighter's spark
not one single star
and even the moon had vanished.

Encounters

Strange, I thought, *why is my son leaning over my bed at three in the morning?*

Then I noticed the pale, otherworldly glow around the figure's head and torso – this was definitely not my son. The charcoal gray form hovering over me stood out against the blackness that filled the rest of the room. A deep terror crawled across my skin and through my soul, like I'd been kissed by a demon.

I screamed, and the apparition faded away into the darkness.

My husband, ripped instantly from peaceful dreams, asked what was happening. Shaking, I told him I saw a figure leaning over the bed, but it was gone now. He asked if it was a large shadow about the size of our son. My heart stopped. I answered yes. He confided that a figure fitting that description was lingering at the foot of our bed a couple weeks ago. He hadn't said anything, because he didn't want to upset me.

That was my first encounter with a spirit.

***

A few years ago, I walked into Walmart with my disabled child sitting in the grocery cart. A

Latino man walked over to us, laid a hand gently on my son's head, and asked if he could pray for him. Startled, I nodded my head. He prayed for Jo's health and for our family to be given strength.

Astonishingly, Jo made no attempt to move away from the stranger's hand. When the man finished praying, he smiled at me and said, "he's going to be okay." I smiled down at Jo and looked up to thank the stranger for his kindness.

He was gone.

We were in a wide-open area at the front of the store. Even if he'd been running, he couldn't possibly have gotten out of my field of vision that quickly.

That was my first encounter with an angel.

***

Late one night, when my kids were little, I sat at my computer desk in the basement. Back then, social media revolved around message boards. I was joking around with some friends online while my kids slept and my husband was at work.

A familiar voice right next to me broke the silence. "You better go check on your boy." It was my grandfather.

My grandfather, at that time, had been dead for ten years.

His face was shadowy but recognizable as it floated about two feet to my left. "Floated" isn't exactly the right word; it was more like he was peeking in from somewhere else. A golden light shown behind him, but it wasn't spotlighting him, it was filling up the space behind him. As soon as I looked at him full on, he was gone.

I didn't disobey my grandfather as a child, and I wasn't about to start now. I ran upstairs and peeked into Jo's room. He was struggling to breathe.

I repositioned him, and he began breathing normally.

He's now being treated for severe sleep apnea. I don't know what would've happened if Grandpa hadn't intervened, but I have a pretty good guess.

That's how I know there's an afterlife.

**

One night I began watching a nature documentary on TV. The evening was peaceful; Jo played contentedly in his Pack 'n Play, my older son was spending the night with his grandparents, and my husband was at work.

The peace was shattered by food poisoning. I became very sick, very quickly. I began vomiting uncontrollably. Soon afterward I fell unconscious on the living room floor.

James' regular shift ended at 11 p.m., but he had a feeling something was wrong.

He left work at 10 p.m., an hour early.

He came home and found me, still unconscious, with a mouth full of vomit. He called 911, and an ambulance rushed me to the hospital, where the emergency room doctor and nurses pumped my stomach.

The doctor, whom they hadn't yet spoken to, came to the waiting room afterward. He told my husband, "You're lucky you found her when you did. An hour later, she'd have been dead."

That was my first encounter with a miracle.

***

People interpret events in their own way. Everyone has their own point of view and their own belief system. Life experiences change our perception of the world around us. Some people seem to be "wired" to believe in and experience supernatural events more than others do.

I, for one, believe in the existence of ghosts, angels, the afterlife and miracles.

EMOTIONAL FUCKERY

Explanation of the End

Perhaps naivete played a role
Couldn't be trusted to grasp common sense
Without bad intentions, she doled out offense
Somehow forgiveness was never the goal

Now that the End is looming near
You'd think that somehow transgressions
Would not be allowed to promote depression
Perhaps it's all coming from fear.

She follows the Good Book and obeys its words
She has tried to make right as it says she should
Her efforts, rejected, she's done what she could.
So she washes her hands of their hateful absurdity.

Perilous Gloom

Whenever I sit
in the late afternoon,
alone in my silent room,
away from the sounds
of voices of hate,
but not from the perilous gloom,
I can almost believe
if I close my eyes
and really, really, try,
that there is a reason
in spite of it all
not to surrender and die.

Vault of Ice

I knock
but I find the door's been locked
from the other side

I try to leave
but all the exits have been blocked

Your overreaction
has isolated the solution
deep inside a vault of ice

The overheated key comes with
a price.

Blame

You always seem to need it
weaponize it
to legitimize what you don't understand

Hand in hand with misconceptions
all it does is add to all the things
that started out as wrong
and never healed.

With all your sympathizing,
fake attempts at understanding
you cannot make simple
rational
sense out of what I need

So I bleed

Suffer needlessly

and your interpretation
is I *choose* to live this way*??*

What can I say
when you still believe

that my perceptions
come from a mind so damaged,
reality's in question?

when you use blame to perpetuate
this small misunderstanding?

You insist on moving forward
like we never had to stop,
but I am frozen
and unwilling to move on.

Always Rage

Always rage inside your eyes
ready to antagonize
Evil words wait on your lips
Venom on your fingertips
Late at night you creep about
waiting till the lights go out
You reach for your gleaming knife
and rid the world of one more life.

You Don't Know

You don't know I see you there.
I can't help but smile and stare.
You're completely unaware
that I
burned your office to the ground
emptied out your bank account
since you told me not to come
around.
I hid your towels in a cave
Your dog's in the microwave
Been in there since yesterday
on high
Gave your car an acid wash
Tangled up your dental floss
Drowned your fish in wads of moss
But wait...
Your daffodils will not survive
I erased the files on your hard drive
I sure hope that you and I
stay friends!

DECK OF CHARACTERS

The Medium

Hidden away,
tucked between obscure buildings in a forgotten
part of the city,
is a shabby alleyway,
where a tabby cat marks his territory,
rats scamper toward spoiled food spilled from an
overflowing dumpster, and
a dog whines as he looks up at the full moon.
Animals know that magic has not left this world.

Clutching his treasures,
a Medium on an odyssey from some other place
hesitates, doesn't move,
watches from a temporary doorway by the
dumpster, observes,
studies,
carefully ignores the deal going down
between a man in an expensive leather jacket
and a woman, dripping sweat,
so desperate for a hit
she's practically convulsing.

Instead, the Medium watches a young man arrange
a bed of newspapers so he doesn't have to sleep
directly on the filth that covers the ground.

The Medium turns his head and sees garbage
blowing around,
rearranging itself in the wind.
The Medium fears that magic has left this world.
As he surveys the scene,
absorbing the unfolding actions of a crumbling
society,
he sends vibrations into countless crystal balls.

The Prisoner

In the castle where they keep him
he waits with frightening patience;
Another Empire steals his power
to conquer foreign nations.
Escape is not his plan,
because he has nowhere to go.
Revenge does not occur to him
He'd never sink so low.
He has an understanding
of truths they'll never grasp.
He'll use it to unravel them
from future back through past
Inside the mind they tortured,
behind the eyes abused,
an unsuspected talent
waits calmly to be used.
Once he executes his plan,
he'll stay inside the castle.
Escaping from another dungeon
is just too much hassle.
They'll come and he'll destroy them
in a way they cannot fathom.
He'll touch them with destructive force
and decimate their atoms.

The Traveler

The traveler flows

through a lattice of worlds

He is hurled

through the future

the present

the past

then arrives

in a place without time.

At last.

The Guardian

All the misery
fear
of life and of passion,
felt in one single instant and
silently dismissed.

Information flows rapidly through the sensory
channels of
the Guardian:
the visions, the horror of pain and the miracle of
peace, the ability to heal;
and all are left untouched.

The Guardian tastes centuries passing,
and smells all things finite.

He feels and knows life in every way, but is
powerless to prevent the Universe from flinging
itself through time.

The Guardian knows what it means to walk on
light.

The Warrior

Forever.
Anything's possible here
in the barren land that
just lets time disappear.
As the tears eternally fall from the spear
of the heart hunting warrior,
his deep rotting fear
blackens the soil where his victims' graves grow
row after row after row
after row
He's drawn to the sea that's laced silver with souls
He calls to the moonlight to challenge its glow
Through his victims' tombs
a living wind blows
and the corpses revolt
when the Warrior goes.

The Creator of Alien Worlds

The creator of alien worlds
is trapped in a tower of dreams
built by his severed mind
which Destiny seeks to unwind.
He cries out to the comfort of Nothing
The darkened abyss envelops him
Destroying the shadows and light
and hiding him deep in the night.

In Time, He Waits

He waits.
When I enter that cavern
deep underground,
I can feel his icy breath on my skin.
In the air looms the presence
I know as his essence.
He's waiting for me to release him.
His voice beckons me
subliminally
from the emptiness where a lone spider spins.
Inside of him hides the soul
of a man lost in Time
He tries to follow, catch hold when I leave.
His desperation
sends him fumbling for a world he doesn't know
doesn't understand
never did
and never can.
Still, he jumps for the doorway, just once
but he tumbles back
to the groping hands of forever
mercilessly
And so, in Time,
he waits.

A FEW WORDS ABOUT WORDS

Character

Maybe I'm biased.
But I'll tell you about an interesting freak of nature,
whose timeless existence burns in the torrid flames
of an ocean of fire.

Scorching waves crash around him, bending the
echoes of screams till the air is saturated with
smoky silence.
One could drown or burn as they focus on the story
of the beautiful suffering soul.

She drowns in the hurricane force of his touch, I
type, and delete it immediately.

A volcanic, ethereal reproduction
created to rival the Character's power,
cannot reproduce the magic of him.
Neither can chimes
squirming in the wind

This powerful Presence that lurks in my mind,
hides inside
I'm trying to find him
connect with him

channel him
see what his plans hold for mine

I ripple through temporal fluid and
tidal forces that feed
inspiration,
trying to reach him.

But somehow I am
tethered here.
The need for his reality to burn through blank
pages and scream out his story has chained me to
yearning and impossibility
and will not let me move on.

He deserves more
than existence
as a character in an unwritten story.

Poetry that Rhymes

I constantly search for

She sighs heavily and starts again.

I will scream into the sky
and hear echoes from the stars

I will look into the Universe
through darkness, deep and scarred

Into unknown lands and ages past
and swallowed gulps of Time

I'll taste the empty, frozen land
upon which giants climb.

She reads her words.

I hate poetry that rhymes, she thinks disgustedly,
and flings her pen to the ground.

Lost in the Story

Even after I throw the book down,
hiding the pages between the covers,
slamming the door to that world,
I cannot escape the story.
Lips bloody, jaw swollen,
I grab fistfuls of hair
and cut it
—ten inches gone—
hoping to draw my attention away
hoping for diversion
from the horror unleashed in unsettling worlds
from the hints of finality lurking in those words.
A new reality constructed
and while I'm distracted
I gracelessly fall down the stairs to my death.
I wake up in the book
to discover I've become the villain,
I've become the author.

Cannon

Within some books hide a cannon
which fires words relentlessly when pages are
exposed
Streams of printed words are
hurled toward my eyes
but
before they find my brain, they split in half
And every streaming sentence
will go left
or will go right
Somewhere behind me they'll reunite
before dissipating in the distance
too far for me to reach them.
Traitors to books, those cannons.

Just Words

Just words.
Thousands
Millions
Infinit-illions

struggling so hard
to command my attention

Some screeching angrily,
forcing their colors on me from
the sea of billboards littering the interstate
like insects forcibly drawn to the light
masters of temptation
in every language
beneath neon tubes
glowing green in the night.

Just words
some try breathing their way into my conscious self
so that I might grasp them and write them on paper
or shout them to anyone willing to listen.
Those poor words.
So distressed when I turn them away.

Pages

Beware the realm you wish to enter!
Braver hearts than yours have tried
to venture through unscathed,
unbroken
falling down to utter ruin
Dreamers have been lining up for centuries
in hope of finding
just this place—
It's not for the faint of heart!
Along the path, sometimes, wait monsters
eaters of unwary souls
Merciless and vicious
They'll grip you, they won't let go.
They'll pull you deep into the muck
With any luck
the heroine or hero
has the power to hold the monster back
so you don't become a snack
and spoil the happy ending.

BATTLE

Hazy, gray clouds slid away from me in opposite directions. As I fought my way back to consciousness, they faded into a blurry view of white walls, a nurse's station, and medical personnel. Waking up in a recovery room was nothing new to me. I've had lots of surgery over the years.

I was shivering but didn't feel cold. I didn't feel anything, I realized. Blissful, blessed pain medication flowed through plastic tubing into my bloodstream, but I'd still expected to feel some discomfort. Surgery is never painless, no matter how many drugs they give you.

Four angry red incisions crossed my chest, marking the removal of two and a half pounds of my body.

I pulled the pink linen blanket up to my chin. No one noticed I was awake, so I easily slipped back into comfortable nothingness.

***

Six months earlier

I'd regained consciousness after jaw surgery to the sound of inhuman wailing and a recovery room nurse demanding loudly and urgently that someone find the Dilaudid and find it right now! *A male voice replied to her, sounding almost panicked: The manufacturer of Dilaudid was in Puerto Rico, and their production plant was hit by Hurricane Maria. There was none of the strong narcotic pain medication in the building.*

Guess the wailing person was screwed, I thought.

***

I nestled into the meager blanket. My teeth clacked together so hard I thought they'd shatter.

"I ca-aan't s-st-stop sh-shiv-shiver-vering," I told the nurse. My body was vibrating like strummed guitar strings.

"When you came out of surgery," she replied, "you were shaking the whole bed."

The patient in the bed next to mine was wheeled out of the recovery room. He was awake and feeling well.

My eyes fell shut.

Time passed.

Voices startled me out of oblivion.

"Are you thinking neuro-malignant hypothermia?" someone asked in the dimly lit area near the end of the bed.

That sounds bad, I thought dispassionately. But it also sounded kind of interesting, the way animal documentaries or tours through a museum are interesting. I rolled away from the two whispering nurses and went back to sleep.

The irritating BLEEP-BLEEP-BLEEP of the monitors woke me up as soon as I'd drifted off again. If colors made noise, the blaring alarm would sound neon blue. I didn't like it.

"Jayce, this is definitely not normal," the nurse by my bed called over her shoulder. "I think we should call the anesthesiologist."

"What've you got?" the other woman asked, walking over.

I twisted in the bed, sluggishly fighting the blankets to see what they were looking at.

As they studied my vital signs displayed in bright colors on the computer screen, I tried to focus on them, too.

Blood Pressure: 177/120. That was obviously a faulty reading. My blood pressure had never been that high.

Heart Rate: 163. Bullshit. My pulse didn't race like that anymore, not since my heart surgery three years ago.

Oxygen saturation: 93%. Eh, could be better, could be much, much worse. At least that number seemed plausible.

A new patient, IV pole in tow, was wheeled into the space next to mine.

Sometime later, the anesthesiologist appeared from behind the neutral-toned curtain at the end of my bed. "What's her temperature?" he asked.

"38 degrees," the so-far-nameless nurse answered promptly.

I tried to remember the conversion from Celsius to Fahrenheit from the science classes I took in college, but the fog surrounding my brain made that impossible.

"Give her some Valium," ordered the doctor.

"Did you say Valium?" the nurse repeated, seeming hesitant.

"Yes, and more Demerol."

Valium? I thought. *Great.* I already felt like there were fingers in my head stirring around my brain matter. Now he wanted to give me a tranquilizer? Did he think my symptoms were caused by anxiety? I'd mentioned to him before surgery that I'd had a panic attack last time I woke up from an operation. Did he think my shaking was a panic attack? I was barely even *awake*.

I knew from bitter experience; telling a doctor about any kind of mental health-related response could be a huge mistake. I was furious that I'd done something so stupid.

***

As I lay in the recovery room after jaw surgery, a kind-hearted nurse put her hand in mine for comfort. The screams of the person wailing in the background intensified, and I wanted to yell at Lungs to shut the hell up.

The staff had obviously failed to find Dilaudid.

Too bad you can't get a private recovery room, I thought.

Only seconds later, a male voice said, "You have to let go!" I didn't know what he wanted me to let go of. I felt thick, strong hands struggling to pry my fingers away from the nurse's hand. I wanted to help, but I couldn't remember how to stop squeezing.

Someone appeared with a syringe full of Dilaudid.

"Thank God," the nurse said quietly.

She must've been sick of hearing the screaming, too.

***

I woke to the sound of apprehensive voices once again discussing my vital signs. My bottom blood pressure reading had plunged into the thirties.

"Get the anesthesiologist back up here," Jayce demanded.

"I have to pee," I told her.

A giant vampire bat flew from right to left just below the ceiling in the recovery room. How strange, I thought, that it wasn't using its wings to fly. It just glided along at a steady pace. How was it staying aloft without flapping its wings? How had a *bat* gotten into the hospital in the first place?

I shook uncontrollably, cold but not cold.

***

As I slowly became coherent after my jaw surgery (kind of hard to stay asleep with the constant howling – good lord *somebody needed to put that poor bastard out of their misery) - I noticed how many people were lingering around my bed. A woman stood by my IV administering Fentanyl and speaking to a man who was advising her on the dosage. Two male doctors stood ominously at the end of the bed, watching me. I got the feeling they were supervisors, or maybe administrators of some kind. A young man took my temperature, and another nurse waited behind him. The left side of my jaw felt like I was delivering a flaming, six-armed baby covered with razor-sharp spikes for skin through my mouth. That, at least, would explain all the attention I was getting.*

I realized the screaming person in the recovery room was me.

***

The anesthesiologist again materialized at the end of my bed. In frantic, jumbled English I informed him I wasn't panicking. I didn't need Valium. I told him the only reason I panicked after surgery last time was because I was in intense pain. I obviously wasn't panicking now, I told him, because I hadn't broken anyone's fingers yet.

After a noticeable pause, he said Valium was also used as a muscle relaxer.

He then popped up by the nurses next to the monitors on the other side of the bed. *Woah*, I thought with awe, *he can teleport.* I wanted to compliment him on this extraordinary ability, but the words leaving my brain got lost on the way to my mouth. I looked beyond the small group huddled by my bed. It seemed I was the only patient left in in the recovery room.

"What time is it?" I managed to ask.

"4:30," Jayce answered distractedly.

"How long was my surgery?"

"It lasted about an hour and a half."

Ok, I knew my surgery started at 11:15. That meant it was over by around 12:45. I'd been in recovery almost four hours? My other recovery room stays lasted between forty-five minutes and an hour and a half.

Something was wrong.

"What's going on?" I asked. The nurses and doctor ignored me while they discussed me.

"Tell me what's happening!" I demanded, louder this time.

The anesthesiologist looked up and stared at me silently.

"*What is going on?*" I yelled.

The anesthesiologist walked back around to the other side of my bed. Why didn't he teleport? It pissed me off that he walked.

"We think it's serotonin syndrome."

"What does that mean?" I asked through my still-clacking teeth.

"The levels of serotonin in your brain are too high," he answered tonelessly.

"And what does *that* mean?" I tried to project the image of an angry, swearing face emoji directly into his brain, so he'd know my exact opinion of him.

"It's why your eyes are dilated, and it's causing your fever and shaking."

What was he talking about? My eyes didn't *feel* dilated.

"I have a fever?" I asked skeptically. Weird, I never ran a fever. I once had pneumonia in both lungs and didn't run a fever. My body temperature always sat at a cool 97.4 degrees.

"How high is my fever? In Fahrenheit?"

"About 100.5 degrees," the doctor responded.

Huh, I thought. *No shit.*

After hearing this revelation, I fell back to sleep.

***

Present day

I'm not embarrassed to admit I screamed after jaw surgery. A lot. Spitting out a spiked, flaming baby probably would've hurt less than that procedure.

At first, the surgery appeared to be successful. The doctors removed the discs from both of my temporomandibular joints. They'd slid completely away from where they should've been. I remember the doctor pointing to a couple of white smudges on the radiology film and saying, "See this? It should be over there. And this one? It should be here."

Not only were the discs in the wrong places, they were irreparably damaged. Removing them would keep my jaw from sliding out of place.

While recovering, I was given enough drugs to supply a small cartel. After Fentanyl, Dilaudid, Morphine and Tramadol, I should've been extraordinarily happy . . . and I was. The pain gradually subsided. I went home the day after surgery.

My ability to eat corn-on-the-cob and dried banana chips returned over time. I even lost a few pounds while recovering from surgery. Of course, I promptly gained them back when I could start eating normally again.

To this day I don't know where the Dilaudid came from.

***

"Send her up to intensive care," the anesthesiologist ordered. I wasn't really sure why a mild fever and some shakiness warranted intensive care. On the other hand, I'd never been admitted to the intensive care unit before, and hey, I was always down for new experiences.

Serotonin syndrome, I found out later, can cause coma, seizures, and death. It may have also been responsible for the appearance of a bat flying across the recovery room.

The intensive care unit was quiet, dimly lit, and warm. The nurses were attentive and friendly. My glass stayed full of fresh ice water, and orange Jell-O was delivered on demand. Apparently, I 'demanded' so much I exhausted their supply, and they had to start raiding the Jell-O stashes on other floors.

The surgeon stopped in to check on me. She informed me the serotonin syndrome was a result of my "having too many psych meds on board." Even with a system full of pain meds, I got the message. Clearly, it wasn't the anesthesiologist's fault that I almost died. It was mine, for taking the prescription medication necessary for my mental health, medication I'd listed on my intake forms and reminded them of before they took me back to surgery.

Luckily, I had no lasting physical effects from the serotonin syndrome. I've wondered about the bat I saw in the recovery room a few times, though. In my mind, I've named it "Battle."

UNHINGED

Apocalypse

The world's become so desolate
since everything went wrong
No buildings roads or children playing
Everything is gone
The mountain tops bleed black with death
The wounds will never heal
The last remnants of golden weeds
are falling in the fields
A lonely wind blows everywhere
beneath the fading sky
The last of all still breathing air
wait anxiously to die.

Twinesthesia

The violent, malicious taste of colors
bounced throughout her mouth.
What alien hand
walked its fingers through her mind
and dared to drag The Feeling
like a blanket over her consciousness?
The intended world
flowed slowly out of reach.
Mortified, she watched it slip away.

Heat bounced around the room
in red, velvet waves
and he could not summon the strength
to seek the cool refuge.
The intended world,
the only thing that mattered,
flowed slowly out of reach.
Across the void, he saw
the hand of God

The twins, rejected,
like all that was,
shriveled up, crumbled to ash
and blanketed the earth.

Plight of the Almost Dead

Loving you is killing me
I don't wanna live in a cemetary
I don't wanna go to a mortuary
and have some mortician's hands all over me.

I don't wanna be underground in a casket
or summoned with a Ouija board and a planchette
or put in an urn with no view whatsoever.
Don't mess with my ghost or I'll haunt you forever.

Umbrellas in the Bathtub

There's umbrellas in the bathtub
a spider on the wall
Someone broke the toilet and
there's cat puke in the hall
There's a dead fish in the fish bowl
No one's done the dishes
The stove smells kind of funny
and the fridge is downright vicious.
The garbage is decaying
Something's growling in the closet
I just saw my sheets move
Vines are growing from the faucet
There are fifteen broken windows
out of sixteen, that's just sad
The carpet's growing fingers
and the walls are painted plaid
Something's roaring in the basement
Haven't seen my dog in days
There's a monster on my bed
and the ceiling's gone away
Spores and fungus grow unchecked
inside my coffee cup
The chairs are floating upside down
Could someone wake me up?

Decaying

I was decaying under the bed
when along came my sister and yanked off my
head. She took it away, I have not seen it since
The rumor mill tells me
it's under a fence.
Worms have long since chewed my lips
They drank my brain fluid in delicate sips.
Never again can I blow my nose
and hide the snot in my brother's clothes.
At least, no more zits
with which to deal!
They gave the worms a tasty meal.

Light on the Eve of Creation

To touch you is light on the Eve of Creation.
Before the expanse that created damnation,
I reach through the depths while you shimmer
beside me
as thousands of stars are exploding inside me.

Underground

Underground,

demon religions

All have been slaughtered

but all is forgiven

Tell my why

and how did I

get here?

Red light from down

in the dungeon

One more fool

goes crashing under

Empty screams ask,

Why am I still here?

Alarm

In the place of serenity,
there's upheaval by nature.
Where peace has been provided,
the alarm keeps going off.

From the bluest shining sky,
the blackest storm drops down to earth.
And the peaceful, sleeping child
awakens screaming in the night.

The disturbance in the city
is ignored by jaded minds
The bravest and the ignorant
share a single place in line

in the silent halls of midnight.
The alarm keeps going off and
the weeds keep growing
larger in the garden.

The Price of the Deal

A wrinkled old woman with nowhere to go
waits in her room on the seventeenth floor
Her apartment is empty and so is her mind
She stares past gray walls at the black moonless
night.
What she sees there is strange, but she isn't afraid
She's known since the deal it would happen
someday:
An army of specters, faceless and dark
breaks into her room and feasts on her heart.

Dastardly Deed in the Mailbox

A dinosaur cried in my mailbox.

Now it is rusted and moldy.

All of my neighbors are angry.

They flutter and bark at me coldly.

Free Intuitive Exercise

Curly children
standing on a straight wave
in a Universe made of solid sound
where brightly colored shapes float in the silver
mist.
Fog turns into blobs of orange gelatinous shapes
turns into blobs of glitter in the sky
The sky can't be seen, of course, only felt
and smelled.
And sensed.
Many sensations emanating from the solid sound
dimension
Many creatures hidden in the air.
Air is fluid, fluid is full of books
explaining how to spiral the dog curls.
Black, shiny black holes
Sucking light out of one Universe
and spitting it out into another.
Energy is converted into crackers, whose purple lips
fall from the sky and land
on ancient telephone books
and stir up a glorious cloud of
Karate.
Asteroids

in my bean bag cause me to swallow
doors
doors which cannot eat, doors which have voices
but can only speak if someone
moves them.
Welcome to the chaotic jungle that exists in my
family.
Vines creeping into the zone of bread and sound
where the leg of my skin creaks open and allows
monsters to enter
and become my toes.

Situation

She was trapped in a bearhug
by a corpse with rigor mortis
The screams were as infinite as the reasons.

Ghost Town

Decaying bodies lounge around.

Lazily, the sun goes down.

There's not a soul to make a sound

as shadows slink through Ghost Town.

No one tries to be discreet.

All the roads are 13th Street.

Creatures who have fifteen feet

go plodding through the ghost town.

Windows break.

Shutters slam.

Invisible train cars ram.

Ask me if I give a damn

I'm floating through Ghost Town.

Every nightmare is a dream,

every day is Halloween

You can struggle, you can scream,

but you'll never leave Ghost Town.

Wall in a Field

There stands a great wall in a field
a portal that speaks to me
revealing a blackening future
while laughing and beckoning me.

I'm wasting time taunting futility
as I look through the pathways of time
The portal reveals the crushed bones
of those who succumbed to the crime.

Monster Droplets

His whole life is dripping
away through the hole

You know that the monster
does not have a soul

You know that the monster
has only one goal:

to gather his droplets
and hide from the troll

Oblivious Bastard

An oblivious bastard
pissed on my toes.
He then shoved his finger
right up his nose.
His finger absorbed
the snot inside.
I saw it myself!
It can't be denied.
He plucked a woman
up off the street.
He felt her up.
She grabbed his meat.
They fucked each other
a foot from my feet.
My shoe melted off
from their passionate heat.

Secrets

Why the Why the Why the Why the

Question? Question? Question?

The answer/answer/answer

I can never, ever mention.

Something I Should Tell You

"Before we start
there's something I should tell you.
I am dead."

"You're *dead*?" he said,
and laughed until his tears fell to the bed.

"I'm dead."
My words, repeated,
echoed down the marble hall,
a calm and silent place
until filled with his death call.

And with his death,
I find that I am still not satisfied.
A beast cannot enjoy a death
unless the man has tried.

Gold Cats

On the rarest of dark nights,

out from the trees

flies the silver owl.

Drawn to the twisted remains of a plane:

a crop duster,

flipped when he dipped far too low.

The owl gathers gold cats

to his strange convention.

There he assigns their futures

he doles out the fate of each cat in the group

he chooses the actions of singular factions

and sends them out into primordial soup.

All My Deaths

I was laying on the beach
worshipping the sun
when I began to realize
that I was all alone.
Sharp colors were spilling,
red and orange,
across the sky.
A mushroom pointed out to me
it was my fate to die.
All other human beings
had vanished from the earth
I heard a distant moaning noise
My head began to hurt
The ground began to shake and swirl
The dead began to rise
I tried to run away
but started floating toward the sky
I thought I'd float to safety
disappear without a trace
But a thousand corpses filled the sky
corpses with my face.

Foresight

Inside the fiery temple,
built to worship foreign gods,
I touched the Ancient book
that sat above the glowing pods
I fell back as I was overcome
with strange hallucinations
Then the future fell before me
with all its strange temptations.

The Death of Time

We saw the whole thing happen
What a senseless pointless act!
The impact was tremendous,
caused a loud resounding splash.

There was no apparent reason
for the drowning that we know;
no sadness or depression
that would make it want to go

What cause for self-destruction?
What reason, death to meet?
Perhaps the Clock felt old,
forgotten, obsolete

We'll never understand, I guess
what pushed it to the brink
or why it chose to end its life
and dive into the sink.

Carnival

Don't know how I'm supposed to feel

Met you on a Ferris wheel

and you puked up your last meal on me

We went on a different ride

You passed out

I let it slide

You fell off the Tilt-O-Whirl and died

So I picked up your fresh corpse

put it on a carousel horse

And moved on to the games

without remorse.

Next

After the destruction
in the midst of dying flames
I'm surrounded by the feeling
that I've finally reached the end
of the journey I began.

www.ingramcontent.com/pod-product-compliance
Lightning Source LLC
Chambersburg PA
CBHW031958040426
42448CB00006B/403